CAUSES AND CONSEQUENCES

CAUSES AND CONSEQUENCES

SIMON ADAMS

W

FRANKLIN WATTS

LONDON·SYDNEY

Designer Thomas Keenes
Editor Constance Novis
Art Director Jonathan Hair
Editor-in-Chief John C. Miles
Picture Research Diana Morris

© 2004 Franklin Watts

First published in 2004
by Franklin Watts
96 Leonard Street
London
EC2A 4XD

Franklin Watts Australia
45-51 Huntley Street
Alexandria
NSW 2015

ISBN 0 7496 5151 2

A CIP catalogue record for this book
is available from the British Library.

Printed in Malaysia

Picture credits

Imperial War Museum/Topham Picturepoint:
front & back cover, 19
Imperial War Museum/TRH Pictures: 17
Peter Newark's Pictures: 2, 9, 10, 13, 25
Popperfoto: 21
Topham Picturepoint: 28b
TRH Pictures: 14

*Every attempt has been made to clear copyright.
Should there be any inadvertent omission, please
apply to the publisher for rectification.*

Artwork

Lee Montgomery, Steve Noon,
Peter Visscher, Mike White

CONTENTS

EUROPE IN 1900

In 1900 the map of Europe, and of the world, looked very different to how it looks today. A handful of nations dominated the continent and controlled vast empires that stretched around the globe. Europe itself had largely been at peace since 1871, but it was far from united.

BRITAIN AND FRANCE

In the early 1800s, first Britain and then France and other nations had undergone a massive industrial revolution. This brought immense wealth as new factories were built and new technologies developed. Both nations had acquired vast overseas empires – Britain in Canada, the West Indies, Africa and India and France in Africa and southeast Asia. These empires often brought Britain and France into conflict.

ITALY AND GERMANY

Until the 1860s, both Italy and Germany consisted of small, independent states. Italy united first, followed a decade later by Germany. Both attempted to catch up economically and militarily with Britain and France. In addition, Italy and Germany wanted to build their own empires. Germany went on to found colonies in Africa and the Pacific. The newly created Germany, however, had many enemies, especially France, which it had fought and defeated in 1870-71, seizing its two eastern provinces of Alsace and Lorraine.

"Place in the hands of the King (Kaiser) the strongest military power, then he will be able to carry out the policy you wish ... through blood and iron."

Otto von Bismarck, 1886

OTTO VON BISMARCK

Otto von Bismarck (1815-98) was born into a wealthy Prussian land-owning family. He entered politics in 1847 and in 1862 became prime minister of Prussia. He reformed and strengthened the army, enabling Prussia to defeat Denmark (1864), Austria (1866) and then France (1870-71). In this way he succeeded in uniting the whole of Germany under Prussian leadership.

As chancellor of this new German empire, Bismarck avoided any more wars in order to build Germany up into a rich, industrial state with colonies in Africa and the Pacific. By the time of his retirement in 1890, Bismarck had created the strongest, most powerful nation in Europe.

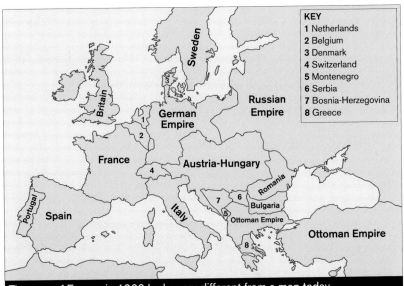

KEY
1 Netherlands
2 Belgium
3 Denmark
4 Switzerland
5 Montenegro
6 Serbia
7 Bosnia-Herzegovina
8 Greece

The map of Europe in 1900 looks very different from a map today.

EASTERN EUROPE

Eastern Europe was almost entirely controlled by three vast empires. For centuries, the Turkish Ottoman Empire had governed most of the Balkans in southeastern Europe, but as its power weakened throughout the 19th century, both Russia and Austria-Hungary eyed these Balkan territories. This created instability and conflict throughout the region.

Although united under the rule of the Habsburg emperor, Francis Joseph I, Austria-Hungary was seriously divided between its many different nationalities, notably Germans, Czechs and Hungarians. Its emperor was old and its government weak. The vast empire of Russia, ruled in an autocratic fashion by Tsar Nicholas II, was also weak and divided, despite its growing industrial strength.

In 1900, as the new century began, Europe was at peace. But beneath the surface there were great tensions. As the Ottoman Empire slowly collapsed, other countries struggled for political, military, economic and territorial advantage over each other.

Europe 1861–1900

1861 Unification of Italy under Victor Emmanuel II, king of Piedmont.

1864, 1866 Prussia defeats first Denmark and then Austria-Hungary to become the leading state in Germany; Italy allies with Prussia to gain Venice from Austria.

1867 Austria-Hungary becomes a dual monarchy under Francis Joseph I.

1870–71 Franco-Prussian War leads to the defeat of France and the unification of Germany under Prussian leadership, with Bismarck as chancellor; Germany gains Alsace and Lorraine from France.

1877–78 Russia defeats Ottoman Empire in Russo-Turkish War; Russian gains are then taken away by the other European nations at the Congress of Berlin in 1878; map of the Balkans redrawn as Austria-Hungary occupies Bosnia-Herzegovina; Serbia, Montenegro and Romania become independent.

1884 After a scramble for colonies in Africa, European nations agree at Berlin to divide Africa between them.

1888 Wilhelm II becomes kaiser of Germany.

1890 Bismarck dismissed by Wilhelm II, who now directs German foreign policy.

1898 Britain and France almost go to war over control of the Sudan and the Nile Valley in Africa.

ARMED ALLIANCES

After 1871, the major European nations formed a series of alliances to protect themselves against attack. More than anything else, it was these alliances that led to war in Europe in 1914.

GERMAN FEARS

After German unification in 1871, Bismarck constructed a series of alliances with Austria-Hungary, Italy, Russia and others in order to protect the new German Empire from attack. France in particular wanted to regain its two eastern provinces lost to Germany in 1871. Most of all, Germany feared war on two sides – from France in the west and Russia in the east – and therefore kept on good terms with Russia.

This system of alliances came under great strain during the 1880s, as Austria-Hungary and Russia struggled to gain control over Bulgaria and other Balkan states. In 1894, therefore, Russia changed sides and signed an alliance with France, enabling it to pursue a much more aggressive policy in the Balkans and elsewhere. Germany and Austria-Hungary feared this new alliance, as it meant that they were now surrounded by two hostile nations.

THE ARMS RACE

Britain played little part in all this alliance building, following a tradition of keeping out of European entanglements. The British pursued a policy of "splendid isolation", using its Royal Navy, the world's biggest, to defend its empire and vast overseas trade. However, the growing industrial and military strength of Germany threatened Britain. Between 1870 and 1914, Germany's population doubled, its industrial output quadrupled and it developed an army that was twice the size of the French army and twelve times the size of Britain's. Crucially, Germany also began to build a huge navy.

European Alliances

1879 Germany signs the Dual Alliance with Austria-Hungary to protect each other against a Russian attack.

1881 Germany, Austria-Hungary and Russia sign the Three Emperors' Alliance to keep Russia friendly.

1882 Triple Alliance signed between Germany, Austria-Hungary and Italy, which guarantees Italy's neutrality if the other two are attacked by Russia.

1883 Austria-Hungary, Serbia and Romania sign an alliance to keep peace in the Balkans and prevent Russia destabilising the region.

1886 Russia and Austria-Hungary disagree over the future status of Bulgaria.

1887 Russia begins to fall out with Germany over trade, financial loans and other issues.

1894 Russia deserts both Germany and Austria-Hungary and signs an alliance with France.

1904 Britain and France settle their colonial differences in West Africa, Egypt and elsewhere and sign the *Entente Cordiale*.

1907 Britain and Russia settle their international disputes and sign an entente; the Triple Entente including France is now in place.

HMS *Dreadnought*, launched in 1906, gave its name to a new class of super big-gun battleships.

THE BRITISH RESPONSE

Britain responded to this threat in two ways, firstly by beginning to construct a new, formidable class of battleships named after HMS *Dreadnought*, which was launched in 1906. *Dreadnought* had ten 12-inch guns and a top speed of 21 knots. Germany retaliated by building similar battleships. By 1914, Britain had 19 Dreadnoughts at sea and 13 under construction, while Germany had 13 at sea and 13 under construction.

Secondly, Britain abandoned its policy of neutrality and in 1904 signed the *Entente Cordiale* ("Friendly Understanding") with its old enemy, France. Under this agreement Britain and France began to co-operate. It was not a formal alliance but the *Entente* brought the two countries closer together. Three years later, Britain settled its disputes with Russia. With Russia, France and Britain now working together, Germany's fear of enemies on either side was now being realised.

EDWARD VII

EDWARD VII became king of Britain in 1901 on the death of his mother, Queen Victoria. His family was related to the crowned heads of most of Europe, including Wilhelm II of Germany and Nicholas II of Russia. He used these family ties to try to bring the major nations of Europe together. Edward was particularly fond of France, where he often holidayed, and enjoyed a great reception when he visited Paris in 1903. His smooth diplomacy helped Britain and France sign the *Entente Cordiale* in 1904. For this and other successes, he became known as "Edward the Peacemaker".

RISING TENSIONS

In the years leading up to 1914, a series of international crises strengthened the two main alliances – the Triple Alliance of Germany, Austria-Hungary and Italy, and the Triple Entente of France, Russia and Britain. By 1914, Europe was divided into two hostile camps.

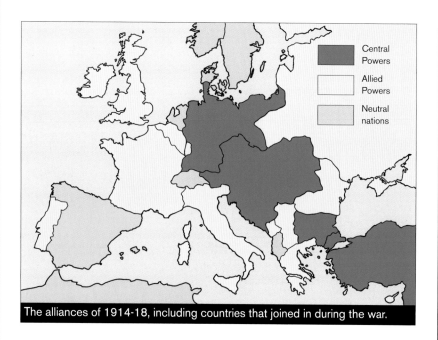

Central Powers

Allied Powers

Neutral nations

The alliances of 1914-18, including countries that joined in during the war.

JAPAN AND MOROCCO

The first two crises occurred outside Europe. In 1904 war broke out between Japan and Russia over control of Manchuria and Korea. Everyone expected the Russians to win, but the Japanese navy crushed Russia's Baltic fleet off the coast of Japan after the Russian ships had sailed halfway round the world. It was the first time a major European power had been defeated by an Asian nation; it was Russia who had to seek peace. Defeat led to widespread discontent inside Russia. The Russian Black Sea fleet and some army groups mutinied. Revolution broke out and it was only put down with much loss of life.

In Morocco, in northwestern Africa, France and Spain agreed in 1904 to divide the then independent

KAISER WILHELM II

WILHELM II (1859-1941) became the kaiser (king) of Germany in 1888 after the death of his father Frederick III; his mother was the sister of Edward VII of Britain. Wilhelm had a strict upbringing and triumphed over his various physical disabilities, including a withered arm. He was, however, very arrogant and quick to take offence. He took great pride in "my navy", as he called the new German fleet, and sought world leadership for Germany. As a result, his military and diplomatic policies alarmed many other nations, notably France and Britain.

In 1914 Wilhelm supported war as he believed it would be short and victorious, but abdicated his throne just before the war ended and went into exile in the Netherlands, where he died in 1941.

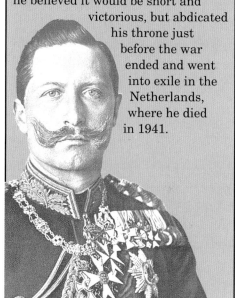

country between them. Germany objected and in May 1905, Kaiser Wilhelm landed in Tangier, northern Morocco, to support the Moroccan sultan. Germany then demanded an international conference to force the French to back down, but it was a diplomatic disaster for them. In 1911 Germany sent the gunboat *Panther* to Morocco to protect its interests in the country. War between France and Germany seemed possible, but Germany eventually backed down and France and Spain divided Morocco between them. In both crises, Britain was alarmed by Germany's aggressive tactics and moved closer to France.

> *"I rejoice. This means peace not only for Bulgaria, but general peace."*

Dr S Daneff, Bulgarian delegate to Treaty of London, 1913

THE BALKANS

In the early 1900s, the Ottoman Empire was on its deathbed. Attempts to reform the chaotic and inefficient government only weakened the country further. Austria-Hungary, which had administered the Ottoman province of Bosnia-Herzegovina since 1878, seized on Ottoman weakness to annexe it fully in 1908. This action was resented by neighbouring Serbia, as many Serbs lived in Bosnia, and by Serbia's ally Russia, which was forced to back down after Germany supported its Austrian ally.

Italy too took the opportunity to grab the Ottoman possessions of Libya in North Africa and the Dodecanese Islands in the Aegean Sea. In 1912 the whole of the Balkans exploded into war as Bulgaria, Greece, Montenegro and Serbia joined together to seize the remaining Ottoman territories in Europe. The Ottoman Empire was left with only a small strip of land around Constantinople, but Bulgaria felt cheated and attacked Greece and Serbia to gain more land. A second peace settlement stripped Bulgaria of most of its previous gains, leaving virtually every country in the Balkans now dissatisfied with their new borders.

World Crises

1904–05 Russia defeated in war against Japan.

1905–06 Mutinies in the Russian Black Sea fleet and army groups lead to revolution in Russia, which is crushed by January 1906; Russian government is seriously weakened.

1905 First Moroccan crisis between Germany and France over control of the country.

1906 International conference at Algeciras, Spain, settles Moroccan crisis in France's favour.

1908 Austria-Hungary annexes Bosnia-Herzegovina.

1911 Germany sends gunboat to Moroccan port of Agadir to protect its interests; France and Germany come close to war, but Germany agrees to French control of Morocco in return for territory in central Africa.

1911 Italy seizes Libya from Ottoman Empire.

1912 France and Spain divide Morocco between them.

1912 Italy takes Dodecanese Islands from Ottoman Empire.

1912–13 First Balkan War ended by Treaty of London; Turkey loses almost all its lands in Europe to Bulgaria, Greece, Montenegro and Serbia.

1913 Second Balkan War ended by Treaty of Bucharest; Bulgarian land given to Greece, Romania, Serbia and Turkey; Albania becomes independent.

SARAJEVO

After the crises of previous years, 1914 started as the most peaceful year for a long time. War in Europe seemed a remote possibility. That illusion was shattered in Sarajevo on 28 June 1914.

THE FATAL SHOT

Archduke Francis Ferdinand, heir to the Austro-Hungarian throne, and his wife, Sophie, Duchess of Hohenburg, were visiting the Bosnian city of Sarajevo to inspect military manoeuvres. Bosnia had only been part of Austria-Hungary since 1908. Many of its Serb peoples resented Austrian rule and wanted to become part of Serbia. A group of six Serbian nationalists took the opportunity to assassinate the archduke in the hope of driving the Austrians out of Bosnia. As the couple drove through the city, one of the nationalists threw a bomb at their car, but it bounced off and exploded behind them. The royal couple were unhurt, but later in the day, as their car took a wrong turning and stopped to reverse, a 19-year-old Bosnian Serb, Gavrilo Princip, leapt out of the crowd and shot the archduke and his wife dead.

MILITARY PREPARATIONS

Austria-Hungary blamed Serbia for the atrocity and began to prepare for war. First, it asked for, and received, an assurance from Germany of its full support for any action it took against Serbia. It then issued an ultimatum to Serbia, which would in effect have ended Serbian independence if it agreed. Serbia was anxious to avoid war and accepted most of the ultimatum, but the Austrian government refused to accept their response and declared war on 28 July.

By this time, the rival alliances in Europe were springing into action. France declared support for its ally Russia, which mobilised its army in support of its ally, Serbia. Germany warned Russia not to mobilise,

THE HABSBURGS

THE HABSBURG FAMILY had ruled Austria since the 13th century, gradually increasing their lands to include a large part of central Europe and the Balkans. Their empire contained many different peoples, and was only held together by the unifying force of the Habsburg crown.

By 1914, the Habsburg emperor, Francis Joseph I, had been on the throne since 1848, and was now aged 84. His private life was tragic: his son and heir, Archduke Rudolph, died in mysterious circumstances in 1889, while his wife Elizabeth was assassinated by an Italian anarchist in 1898. As a result, his great-nephew, Archduke Francis Ferdinand (born in 1863) became heir to the throne.

"The lamps are going out all over Europe; we shall not see them lit again in our lifetime."

Sir Edward Grey,
British Foreign Secretary, 1914

Soldiers arrest Gavrilo Princip shortly after he murdered Archduke Francis Ferdinand of Austria at Sarajevo on 28 June 1914.

Countdown To War

28 June Archduke Francis Ferdinand assassinated in Sarajevo by a Serbian nationalist.

5 July Germany gives Austria a "blank cheque" for action against Serbia.

20 July France pledges support for its ally, Russia.

23 July Austria-Hungary presents ultimatum to Serbia.

25 July Serbia agrees the Austrian ultimatum; Austrian and Serbian armies begin to mobilise.

26 July Russian army mobilises.

27 July France begins military preparations.

28 July Austria-Hungary declares war on Serbia.

30 July General Russian mobilisation.

31 July General Austrian mobilisation; Germany sends ultimatum to Russia to stop mobilisation.

1 August Germany declares war on Russia; general mobilisation in Germany and France.

2 August German ultimatum to Belgium to allow its troops passage; Germany occupies Luxembourg.

3 August Belgium rejects German ultimatum; Germany declares war on Belgium and France.

4 August German troops enter Belgium; Britain declares war on Germany.

but when it refused, declared war against Russia the following day. By now, Germany was concerned that Russia's ally, France, might declare war against it, and so prepared to attack and defeat France in a knock-out blow. Germany occupied tiny Luxembourg and asked Belgium to allow German troops to pass through their country on their way into northern France. When Belgium refused, Germany declared war on both Belgium and France.

In this rush to war, Britain had tried and failed to find a peaceful settlement to the crisis. But when Germany invaded Belgium, Britain was forced to act in defence of Belgian neutrality, which it had guaranteed by treaty since 1839. It therefore declared war on Germany on 4 August. The war in Europe had begun.

1914

The outbreak of war in August 1914 caused a massive mobilisation of men and equipment across the whole of Europe. At first the war moved swiftly and armies covered great distances, but in western Europe the situation soon changed into one of almost permanent stalemate.

THE SCHLIEFFEN PLAN

Germany's constant fear about war in Europe was that it would be attacked on two fronts – from Russia in the east and France in the west. Of the two, Germany feared Russia more, because of its large army and its vast territory and population. Alfred von Schlieffen, German chief of general staff from 1891 to 1905, therefore devised a plan to knock France out of any war first before turning to attack the Russians. This plan required Germany to invade France through the flat plains of Belgium and then sweep round the north and west of Paris.

☛ MEN AT ARMS

(1914) = Date of entry into war

The Allies
- Russia (1914) – 12,000,000
- France (1914) – 8,410,000
- Italy (1915) – 5,615,000
- Britain (1914) – 4,970,000
- USA (1917) – 4,355,000
- British Empire (1914) – 3,140,500
- Japan (1914) – 800,000
- Romania (1916) – 750,000
- Serbia (1914) – 700,000
- Belgium (1914) – 267,000
- Greece (1917) – 230,000
- Portugal (1916) – 100,000
- Montenegro (1914) – 50,000
Total Allied forces – 41,387,500

Central Powers
- Germany (1914) – 11,000,000
- Austria-Hungary (1914) – 7,800,000
- Ottoman Empire (1914) – 2,850,000
- Bulgaria (1915) – 1,200,000
Total Central Powers' forces– 22,850,000

Total men at war – 64,237,500

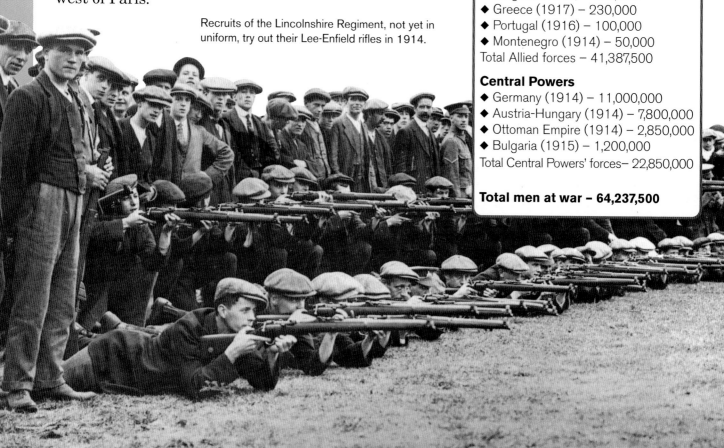

Recruits of the Lincolnshire Regiment, not yet in uniform, try out their Lee-Enfield rifles in 1914.

At first, this plan operated like clockwork. German armies rushed through Belgium, taking Brussels by 20 August. The British sent an expeditionary force to stop the advance but were driven back at Mons, southwest of Brussels. However, as the Germans advanced, they changed their plan and headed straight for Paris. As they did so, they were confronted by the combined French and British armies on the River Marne, east of Paris. Here the advance was stopped, and both sides raced northwards towards the English Channel in an attempt to break through round the side of their enemy's lines. By November 1914, there was stalemate as the two sides dug in along the length of the Western Front, from the English Channel in the north to Switzerland in the south.

"Your country needs you."

British wartime recruitment poster featuring Lord Kitchener, British War Minister

THE EASTERN FRONT

The situation on the Eastern Front against Russia was much more fluid. The Russian army was badly led. It advanced into German East Prussia but was soon surrounded and defeated by the superior German army, first at Tannenberg and then at the Masurian Lakes. The Russians had greater success in Austria-Hungary, however, successfully occupying its eastern province of Galicia.

In the south, Serbia repelled an Austrian invasion. After the Ottoman Empire entered the war in October, a British force from India landed in Ottoman-held Basra in the Persian Gulf and began to advance up through Mesopotamia. British and French empire troops quickly occupied all Germany's colonies in Africa and the Pacific, with the exception of German East Africa (now Tanzania), where fighting continued for the whole of the war. As sea battles raged in the Indian, Pacific and Atlantic Oceans, the war had become truly international.

1914

4 August Germany invades Belgium; Britain declares war on Germany and begins a naval blockade of its ports.
6 August Austria-Hungary declares war on Russia.
12 August Austria-Hungary invades Serbia.
13 August Britain and France declare war on Austria-Hungary.
22 August British Expeditionary Force arrives in France.
23 August–5 September British troops retreat from German advance at Battle of Mons.
26–30 August Germans rout Russians at Battle of Tannenberg.
5–9 September British and French halt German advance at Battle of the Marne.
6–15 September Further Russian defeat at Battle of Masurian Lakes.
8–12 September Russians occupy the Austrian province of Galicia.
18 September–24 November "Race to the Sea" as Allied and German forces try to outflank each other northwards towards the English Channel.
12 October–11 November Inconclusive First Battle of Ypres.
29 October Turkish fleet bombards Russian Black Sea ports.
4–5 November Allies declare war on Turkey.
9 November German cruiser *Emden* sunk by Australian navy in Indian Ocean.
8 December British sink four German ships in Battle of the Falkland Islands.

1915

In August 1914 most people thought that the fighting would "all be over by Christmas". But by the start of 1915, both sides realised they were in for a lengthy conflict. Attempts to break the stalemate – both on the Western Front and at Gallipoli – met with little success.

THE WESTERN FRONT

By early 1915, a line of trenches stretched the length of the Western Front. The two armies were well dug in, exchanging regular artillery fire in the hope of inflicting large-scale casualties and perhaps knocking out an enemy trench and gaining some small advantage. Allied offensives in northern France and Belgium – at Neuve Chapelle in March, Ypres in April and Loos in September – did little to break the stalemate. At Ypres poison gas was used by the Germans for the first time on the Western Front, bringing a deadly new weapon to an already brutal war.

GALLIPOLI

Many Allied strategists looked east to break the deadlock by knocking Ottoman Turkey out of the war. In early 1915 Allied warships attempted to force a way through Turkish naval defences in the Dardanelles – the stretch of water linking the Aegean to the Sea of Marmara and the Black Sea – and take the Ottoman capital, Constantinople, thus driving Turkey out of the war. That failed so a new plan was devised to land troops in

"The earth shook and the air was filled with the thunderous roar of the exploding shells."

British officer describing the offensive at Neuve Chapelle, 10 March 1915

A Turkish soldier at Gallipoli.

KEMAL ATATURK

MUSTAFA KEMAL was born in 1881 in the then Turkish town of Salonika, now part of Greece. He distinguished himself fighting for the Ottoman army against the Italians in Libya in 1911 and against the Bulgarians in 1912-13. At Gallipoli, Kemal was appointed a divisional commander and helped to strengthen the Turkish defences, later leading the 19th Division on the ridges above Anzac Cove and so preventing the Allies from advancing inland.

After the war, Kemal led a revolt to prevent the dismemberment of Turkey as a result of the peace settlement. In 1923 he became the first president of the Turkish Republic, later gaining the name Ataturk, "Father of the Turks".

Australian and New Zealand troops sail towards the Gallipoli peninsula in April 1915.

1915

19 January First German Zeppelin (airship) bombing raids on British ports.

31 January Germans use gas on Eastern Front.

18 February Germans start submarine blockade of Britain.

19 February British and French warships attack the Dardanelles.

8 April Turks begin to massacre and deport Christian Armenians, whom they accuse of collaboration with Russia.

22 April Second Battle of Ypres starts; Germans use poison gas for first time on Western Front.

25 April Allied troops land in Gallipoli.

26 April In the secret Treaty of London, Allies offer Italy extensive territorial gains if it enters the war on their side.

7 May German U-boat sinks *Lusitania* off the coast of Ireland.

23 May Italy joins Allied side.

3 June–18 September Spectacular German and Austrian advances into Russia.

23 June–7 July First of 11 battles take place on Isonzo River.

22 September–6 November Allies launch unsuccessful offensive on the Western Front.

6 October Bulgaria enters war on side of Central Powers and invades Serbia.

Gallipoli, to the west of the Dardanelles, and advance to the capital on land. But the Turks were well prepared. The landings in April and in August were a disaster. The Allied troops – notably the ANZAC (Australian and New Zealand Army Corps) forces – were pinned down on the beaches by Turkish gunfire and many died. In January 1916, the Allies withdrew.

ALLIED REVERSES

Elsewhere, the war was also going badly for the Allies. A German submarine blockade of Britain restricted supplies reaching the country. However, the sinking of the ocean liner *Lusitania* by a German U-boat (submarine) with the loss of many US lives turned American public opinion against Germany. Italy entered the war on the Allied side in May 1915, but its armies soon became bogged down in the first of 11 battles on the River Isonzo. Bulgaria joined the Central Powers in October and invaded Serbia, defeating and occupying both Serbia and its ally Montenegro in January 1916.

1916

War dragged on and both sides needed more men to fight. Britain began conscription. The countries at war also needed ever more munitions and equipment. National economies were now being devoted solely to the war effort. British naval blockades of Germany and German U-boat blockades of Britain led to shortages in both countries.

VERDUN

In early 1916 Germany decided to break the stalemate on the Western Front. The German army could not defeat the British army in northern France, nor invade Britain itself, so Germany decided to attack the French. The intention, as stated by General von Falkenhayn, German chief of general staff, was to make them "bleed to death", thus forcing France out of the war. Its target was Verdun, a well-defended town close to the border with German-held Lorraine. The German attack on 21 February took the French by surprise. At first the French forces retreated, but under General Pétain, they held firm and eventually turned events in their favour. By the time the battle ended in December, there were more than 700,000 French and German casualties.

THE SOMME

In order to take some pressure off the French at Verdun, the British launched a massive attack further north, by the River Somme. After a huge artillery barrage designed to knock out the German defences, British troops clambered out of their trenches on 1 July and advanced towards the German lines. But the barrage had failed to do its work, and the soldiers were mown down by enemy gunfire. More than 60,000 men lost their lives on the first day of the battle, which continued with further massive loss of life until November. The Allies captured about 125 square kilometres of land, but failed to break through.

"What a bloodbath. ... Hell cannot be this dreadful."

Albert Joubaire,
a French soldier at Verdun, 1916

GENERAL PÉTAIN

GENERAL HENRI–PHILIPPE PÉTAIN (1856-1951) joined the French army in 1878 and rose through the ranks to become a general in 1914. He took command of the French forces at Verdun on 25 February 1916, the same day the strategic fort of Douaumont was lost to the Germans as they advanced on the town. He organised the defence of Verdun and made sure the army was properly supplied, raising French morale with his rallying cry, *"Ils ne passeront pas!"* (They shall not pass!)

In May 1917 he became commander-in-chief of the French army, again raising morale when mutinies threatened defeat. He stayed in charge until the war's end.

THE EASTERN FRONT

While deadlock continued on the Western Front, the German army on the Eastern Front had pushed far into Russia, capturing Warsaw and other important cities. But their Austrian allies to the south were weak, a weakness exploited by the Russian general, Brusilov. In June he launched a surprise attack against eastern Austria, capturing large numbers of prisoners and advancing hundreds of kilometres. The attack caused Germany to move troops away from the Western Front to help its ally, as well as encouraging Romania to join the war on the Allied side.

At sea, the only major naval battle of the war was fought in the North Sea, off Jutland. Although inconclusive, it did convince the German fleet to remain safely in port for the rest of the war. In the Middle East, the Arabs in the Turkish-held Arabian Peninsula rose in revolt, helped by a British army officer named TE Lawrence, better known as "Lawrence of Arabia".

British troops in the Ancre (a tributary of the River Somme) Valley in the closing stages of the Battle of the Somme, October 1916.

1916

6 January British parliament votes for conscription.

9 January Final Allied withdrawal from Gallipoli.

21 February–18 December Battle of Verdun rages between Germany and France.

24 April Easter Rising by Irish Republicans against British rule in Ireland.

31 May–1 June Inconclusive naval battle of Jutland.

4 June–20 August Brusilov offensive against Austria-Hungary makes huge gains.

5 June Arabs revolt against Turkish rule.

1 July 60,000 British casualties on first day of Battle of the Somme, which lasts until 18 November.

27 August Romania joins Allies but is overrun and defeated by Austro-German forces in December.

15 September British use tanks for first time during Battle of the Somme.

21 November Emperor Francis Joseph I of Austria dies; his great-nephew Karl succeeds him.

December "Turnip Winter" begins as food shortages cause Germans to use turnip flour in place of wheat flour.

7 December David Lloyd George becomes British prime minister.

1917

For both sides, 1917 was a year of mixed fortunes. Years of war took their toll on every nation, causing revolution in Russia, mutiny in France and the first signs of collapse in Austria-Hungary. Supplies of food became critically short in both Germany and Britain, and the death toll mounted. Neither side had the strength to deliver the decisive blow.

US soldier of 1917.

AMERICA ENTERS THE WAR

Ever since war broke out in 1914, the United States had remained neutral. The country had no wish to get involved in a European conflict, although the sinking of American ships by German U-boats turned US public opinion towards the Allies. In February 1917 Germany announced it would attack all foreign ships, not just Allied, in order to starve Britain out of the war. Germany also tried to divert American attention away from Europe by encouraging Mexico to attack the USA. This was revealed by the publication of a telegram sent by the German foreign minister, Arthur Zimmermann, to his minister in Mexico. The American people were outraged and in April the US government declared war on Germany.

RUSSIA LEAVES THE WAR

As one ally joined, another left. Throughout the war, the Russian army had been led incompetently; its losses had been huge. Discontent with the tsar and his government erupted in the capital, St Petersburg. In March the tsar abdicated and a provisional government was formed. The new government continued the war, but many soldiers deserted, and others refused to fight. In November, a second revolution brought the Bolsheviks to power. They quickly negotiated a ceasefire with Germany.

DAVID LLOYD GEORGE

DAVID LLOYD GEORGE (1863-1945) entered parliament as a Liberal in 1890. He was a radical member of the Liberal government after 1905, introducing old age pensions and other reforming measures.

In July 1915 he was appointed Minister of Munitions in the recently formed coalition government and was very effective at increasing supplies to the Western Front. Secretary of State for War in July 1916, he replaced Asquith as British prime minister in December 1916 and pursued the war energetically, leading Britain to victory in 1918. He attended the Paris Peace Conference in 1919 and did much to shape the post-war peace settlement. He resigned as prime minister in 1922.

"I died in hell – they called it Passchendaele."

Siegfried Sassoon,
British soldier and poet

Russian troops on the retreat in Poland.

THE WESTERN FRONT

On the Western Front, further attempts to break the deadlock in April failed to achieve much. French troops began to mutiny, although Pétain, hero of Verdun, was put in charge of the French army and managed to hold morale together. A further Allied onslaught in July, for the third time at Ypres, led to 250,000 casualties and petered out in a sea of mud around Passchendaele.

OTHER FRONTS

In Italy the final Battle of the Isonzo took place in August. The Italians had advanced only 16 kilometres in 11 battles over two years but had seriously weakened the Austrian army. With Russia, Serbia and Romania out of the war, Germany had troops to spare and after quietly advancing through mountainous territory suddenly attacked the Italians at Caporetto, causing the Italian front to cave in. British and French reinforcements rushed to Italy to save it from collapse. Meanwhile, Arab and British forces continued to attack the Ottoman Empire, taking Baghdad in March and Jerusalem in December.

1917

16 January Zimmermann telegram to German minister in Mexico suggests an alliance with Mexico against USA.

1 February Germany begins unrestricted submarine warfare in Atlantic.

1 March Zimmermann telegram published in USA.

8 March Strikes and riots break out in St Petersburg.

12 March Provisional government formed in Russia; tsar abdicates on 15 March.

24 March Austria's new emperor, Karl, indicates in secret letter to Allies that he is ready to make peace.

April Britain has no sugar and only enough wheat to last six weeks, due to German submarine attacks against merchant shipping.

6 April USA enters the war on Allied side.

9 April Allies attack at Arras; Canadians take Vimy Ridge but fail to break through; further attempts fail on the River Aisne.

17 April French army mutinies.

2 May First Allied shipping convoy in the Atlantic deters German U-boat attacks.

7 June British detonate vast mines under Messines Ridge, causing huge loss of German life.

27 June Greece joins Allies.

31 July–10 November Third Battle of Ypres, also called Battle of Passchendaele.

17 August Final Battle of the Isonzo.

24 October–26 December Italians defeated at Battle of Caporetto.

6 November Bolsheviks seize power in Russian Revolution.

20 November–3 December British use massed tanks at Battle of Cambrai.

3 December Russians and Germans agree ceasefire at Brest-Litovsk.

9 December British troops take Jerusalem.

1918

With Russia now out of the war and US troops entering it, 1918 promised to be make-or-break year. However, it was not until August that it became clear which side was likely to win.

THE LUDENDORFF OFFENSIVE

After the peace treaty with Russia in March 1918, Germany was able to pull its troops away from the Eastern Front and send them to fight in the west. Its main concern there was that large numbers of US troops would soon be arriving in Europe to reinforce the Allies. Therefore, the German commander, General Ludendorff, planned a decisive blow against the still-strong Allied armies, hoping to provoke a French collapse and German victory in the war.

The attack began on 21 March and saw the Germans advance 64 kilometres by 5 April. More gains were made until the advance was halted on 18 July. The Germans were running out of supplies, while the Allies, now under the single command of General Foch and refreshed by more than one million US troops, were ready to fight back.

THE FINAL HUNDRED DAYS

The end when it came was sudden. On 8 August, 456 British tanks rolled forwards near Amiens in northern France, supported by an artillery barrage and massed infantry. Further offensives along the line took the Allies up to the German defensive Hindenburg Line, known to them as the Siegfried Line, by 3 September. Once through, the Allies – Belgian and British in the north, French in the centre and Americans in the south – pushed into territory lost to Germany in the first weeks of the war.

By now, Germany's position was weakening by the day. Their Bulgarian allies collapsed and sued for peace at the end of September, while Italy won a massive

---

FERDINAND FOCH

FERDINAND FOCH (1851-1929) was one of the few Allied commanders who emerged from the war with his stature enhanced. He fought in the Franco-Prussian War of 1870-71 and then became an artillery specialist. In 1914 he commanded the French Ninth Army at the Battle of the Marne and subsequently served in Flanders and on the Somme. After a brief retirement, he came back in 1917 as chief of staff to General Pétain, but he showed more initiative than Pétain and in April 1918 became supreme Allied commander, directing the summer counter-offensive that led to the German collapse.

"No more slaughter, no more mud and blood. ... There was silence along the miles and miles of thundering battlefronts ... It was over."

Lieutenant RG Dixon,
British soldier, 11 November 1918

victory against the crumbling Austro-Hungarian Empire in October. As British and Arab troops pushed north into Syria, the Ottoman Empire too sued for peace. Germany had no allies left, and on the same day Austria-Hungary agreed an armistice with the Allies, the German fleet mutinied at Kiel.

ARMISTICE

By this time, Germany itself was in turmoil. The government had already resigned and the new government, headed by Prince Max von Baden, a cousin of Wilhelm II, began to negotiate peace terms with President Wilson. On 7 November, as a German delegation arrived behind Allied lines to discuss an armistice with General Foch in his railway carriage, revolution broke out in Munich; two days later the kaiser abdicated. Faced with revolt at home, Germany signed the armistice at 5 am on 11 November. It came into effect at 11 am. After more than four years of fighting, the war was over.

A young German surrenders to a British soldier in 1918.

1918

8 January President Woodrow Wilson issues his "Fourteen Points" peace programme.

3 March Russia and Germany sign peace treaty at Brest-Litovsk.

21 March–5 April Major German offensive on Western Front.

14 April General Foch takes over as supreme Allied commander.

27 April–6 June Germans continue to advance during third Battle of the Aisne.

15 July–7 August German advance halted during second Battle of the Marne.

8–11 August British use tanks to punch hole in German lines near Amiens.

21 August Allied offensive pushes Germans back to defensive Hindenburg Line by 3 September.

30 September Armistice between Bulgaria and Allies; German government resigns.

1–2 October British and Arab troops take Damascus in Syria.

4 October Prince Max von Baden becomes German chancellor; both Germany and Austria-Hungary accept President Wilson's Fourteen Points for peace and appeal for an armistice.

24 October Italians win decisive victory over Austrians at Battle of Vittorio Veneto.

28–29 October Austria-Hungary begins to collapse as Czechs and Yugoslavs declare independence.

30 October Allies agree armistice with Ottoman Empire.

3 November Allies agree armistice with Austria-Hungary; German fleet mutinies at Kiel.

9 November Kaiser Wilhelm II abdicates and flees into exile in the Netherlands.

11 November Allies and Germans sign armistice; war ends at 11 am.

THE COST OF WAR

The guns fell silent on 11 November 1918. The world began to add up the full cost of the war. It was a daunting task – the damage had been immense.

NAMING THE WAR

When war broke out in August 1914, it was, at first, fought between European nations, but those nations had colonies in Africa, Asia and the Pacific and navies around the world, which meant that the conflict soon became a world war. At first it was known as the Great War, since there had never been a war like it in human history. But when a second world war began in 1939, a new title came into use – the First World War or World War One – which is how it is usually referred to today.

THE HUMAN COST

The human cost was staggering. About 65 million men fought, of whom 8.5 million died and 21.2 million were injured. These figures are probably an underestimate, as the exact totals will never be known. Millions of young men were killed or maimed for life. Many of these were talented writers, poets, farmers, engineers and industrial workers whose skills their countries would miss in the future.

Most families lost at least one son, cousin or father; some lost all male relatives. Many of those who fought returned with terrible facial and other injuries, and required plastic surgery and artificial limbs to rebuild their shattered bodies. Many others suffered from "shellshock", now known as post-traumatic stress disorder, an illness in which the effects of witnessing so many traumatic events causes mental breakdown.

The impact varied considerably between countries. Of the Romanian soldiers, 44 per cent lost their lives, with another 16 per cent injured. Both Germany and Russia each lost 1.7 million men. In addition to these military deaths were the 6.6 million civilians who died as a result of the war.

THE HUMAN COST

Dead (Wounded)

The Allies
- Russia – 1,700,000 (4,950,000)
- France – 1,357,800 (4,266,000)
- Britain – 743,000 (1,662,600)
- Italy – 650,000 (947,000)
- Romania – 335,700 (120,000)
- British Empire – 206,800 (427,200)
- USA – 48,000 (204,000)
- Serbia – 45,000 (133,000)
- Belgium – 13,000 (45,000)
- Portugal – 7,000 (14,000)
- Greece – 5,000 (21,000)
- Montenegro – 3,000 (10,000)
- Japan – 300 (900)

Total Allied – 5,114,600 (12,800,700)

Central Powers
- Germany – 1,774,000 (4,216,000)
- Austria-Hungary – 1,200,000 (3,620,000)
- Ottoman Empire – 325,000 (400,000)
- Bulgaria – 87,500 (152,000)

Total Central Powers – 3,386,500 (8,388,000)

Total – 8,501,100 (21,188,700)

The huge British cemetery at Tyne Cot, near Ypres, Belgium.

Two million of these deaths were Russians, who died of starvation or as a result of the German occupation of the western part of their country. A further one million were Armenians killed during 1915 by Turkish forces in a campaign of genocide against subject peoples who wanted freedom from Turkish rule.

> *"The cruellest and most terrible war that has ever scourged mankind."*
>
> David Lloyd George,
> British prime minister, 11 November 1918

THE ECONOMIC COST

When war started, no country was prepared for what became a "total war". It was a war of national economies as much as of soldiers, which transformed the lives of everyone. In Britain, as elsewhere in Europe, the government took complete control of the national economy. It set up armaments factories, restricted imports, limited the sale of alcohol in order to reduce drunkenness among workers and even put the clocks forward an hour in summer to increase the working hours of daylight, a change still with us today.

The effect on women was most pronounced. For the first time ever their services were needed in traditional male-only factories to replace the five million industrial workers who had gone off to fight. British women showed their strength and independence by stepping in to fill this massive gap. Apart from gaining a new-found power and freedom, they were rewarded in 1918 when those aged 30 and over finally got the right to vote after years of often militant campaigning.

The total cost of the war was about $186 thousand million: Germany spent $37.7 thousand million; Britain $35.3 thousand million; the USA and France about $24 thousand million each. To pay for this vast spending, taxes were raised and in Britain the national debt increased tenfold, in part paid by loans from ordinary people dipping into their savings.

THE UNKNOWN WARRIOR

DURING THE WAR, the bodies of thousands of soldiers who died in battle were unidentifiable or were missing, presumed dead. Lieutenant-Colonel Henry Williams, a member of the Imperial War Graves Commission – established in 1917 to bury or commemorate the dead of the British Empire – suggested that one unidentifiable body should be reburied in Britain as a symbol of all those others who had no grave.

On 11 November 1920 – two years exactly after the end of the war – the coffin of the Unknown Warrior was carried through London to Whitehall, where George V unveiled the national war memorial, the Cenotaph (from the Greek for "empty tomb"). It was then taken for burial in Westminster Abbey.

France's *Soldat Inconnu* ("unknown soldier") was buried with great ceremony in the Arc de Triomphe in Paris, while in the United States there was a similar burial in Arlington National Cemetery in Washington DC.

THE PEACE TREATIES

Having fought for four years, the Allies now had to make a peace that would last.
The task was complex, and took as long as the war itself to complete.

PEACE AIMS

In April 1917 President Wilson had asked the US Congress to declare war against Germany to make the world "safe for democracy". On 8 January 1918 he made another speech to Congress in which he laid out his Fourteen Points for the post-war world. These included an end to secret diplomacy, freedom of trade and of the seas, a reduction in armaments, the right to national self-determination for all subject peoples and the establishment of an international organisation to promote peace and prevent war. It was an ambitious, even idealistic, programme and it formed the basis of the various peace treaties negotiated after the war.

REDRAWING THE MAP

The war saw the collapse of four large empires and the overthrow of their historic royal families. In Russia, the Bolsheviks had set up the world's first Communist state. The map of Europe was being redrawn as subject peoples like the Czechs declared their independence.

To deal with this chaos, 27 nations met in Paris in January 1919. The four Allied leaders dominated the conference – Woodrow Wilson of the US, David Lloyd George of Britain, Georges Clemenceau of France and Vittorio Orlando of Italy – but they often disagreed. France had suffered most from German occupation and wanted to make Germany as weak as possible. Britain agreed but then came round to the view that a weak Germany would weaken Britain, too, as it would be unable to buy its exports. The US wanted all subject peoples to be given their independence, but Britain and France had empires they did not want to lose. The only thing they agreed on was founding an international peace-keeping organisation, the League of Nations.

> *"The world must be made safe for democracy."*

President Wilson addressing the US Congress, 2 April 1917

PRESIDENT WILSON

WOODROW WILSON (1856-1924) was a professor at Princeton University before being elected Democratic governor of New Jersey in 1910, where he made a name for himself as a reformer. In 1912 he successfully ran for president.

When war broke out in 1914, Wilson kept the US neutral, winning re-election in 1916 on the slogan "He Kept Us Out of War". However, unrestricted submarine warfare by Germany and the Zimmermann telegram (see page 20) led him to declare war in April 1917.

Above all, Wilson wanted to create an international organisation that would guarantee world peace and prevent future wars. But the Senate would not ratify the Treaty of Versailles nor support US membership of the League of Nations. Wilson began to campaign to win support for his ideals but suffered a stroke in September 1919. He stepped down as president in 1921.

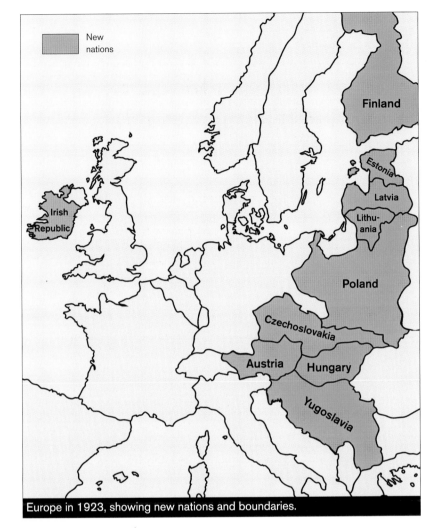

New nations

Europe in 1923, showing new nations and boundaries.

PEACE AT LAST

Eventually, on 28 June 1919, the main peace treaty with Germany was signed in the Palace of Versailles outside Paris. The treaty established German guilt for the war, made it pay substantial war reparations and stripped it of much of its former territory. Further peace treaties with Austria, Hungary and the other defeated nations followed by August 1920, breaking up the old empires, creating new states and making each pay for their role in the war.

Former colonies were given to the victorious Allies but only as League of Nations mandates to be prepared for independence. Only one treaty, with the Ottoman Empire, failed to hold, and after the establishment of a republic in Turkey with Mustafa Kemal – hero of Gallipoli – as president, a new treaty was agreed in 1923.

☛ THE PEACE TREATIES

June 1919
Treaty of Versailles with Germany
- Germany accepts guilt for causing war
- German colonies given to Allies as League of Nations mandates
- Germany returns Alsace and Lorraine to France, and adjusts other borders
- Creates a "Polish corridor" through Eastern Germany to the Baltic
- Rhineland de-militarised and occupied for 15 years
- Germany to pay massive reparations
- German armed services limited in size

September 1919
Treaty of St Germain with Austria
- Creates German-speaking republic of Austria
- Allocates territory to neighbours
- Austria forbidden to unite with Germany – no "Anschluss" (union)
- Austria to pay reparations

November 1919
Treaty of Neuilly with Bulgaria
- Allocates land to Greece and Yugoslavia
- Bulgaria to pay reparations

June 1920
Treaty of Trianon with Hungary
- Reduces Hungary to two-thirds of its previous size and allocates territory to surrounding nations
- Hungary to pay reparations

August 1920
Treaty of Sèvres with Ottoman Empire
- Ottoman Empire loses its Arab lands
- Western Turkey given to Greece. Treaty is rejected by new republican government of Turkey in 1921.

July 1923
Treaty of Lausanne with Turkey
- Rewrites Sèvres and returns Greek gains to Turkey
- Greece and Turkey exchange minority populations
- Recognises new borders of Turkey

THE CONSEQUENCES OF WAR

Although the Allies hoped that the peace treaties would solve the problems of Europe, they were soon disappointed. Within a few years the settlement began to unravel, and Europe headed for war once again.

THE LEAGUE OF NATIONS

President Wilson believed that the League of Nations could prevent war through arbitration and peaceful sanctions against aggressive nations. But the US Senate refused to ratify the Versailles Treaty and join it. The League had some successes, but the absence of the US, Soviet Russia (until 1934), Germany and Japan (both after 1933) weakened its impact.

GERMANY

The main problem was Germany. It had been forced to seek peace, but had not been defeated nor had it surrendered. Many Germans felt humiliated when the

Germans sold worthless bank notes as waste paper in the 1920s.

JOHN MAYNARD KEYNES

MOST PEOPLE THOUGHT that the Versailles Treaty would last, despite its many faults. An exception was John Maynard Keynes (1883-1946), a brilliant economist who attended the peace conference as a British government economic advisor. In his best-selling book, the *Economic Consequences of the Peace* (1919), he argued that the reparations demanded of Germany and her allies would damage the international economy. If Germany was kept poor, he said, it would keep the rest of Europe poor and produce great resentment against the peace treaties and a possible return to war.

Keynes was soon proved right, but the repayment of reparations continued until the financial crash of 1931 brought them to an end.

Allies presented the Versailles Treaty to them and threatened to resume the war unless they agreed all the terms without condition. Many also felt that their army had been "stabbed in the back" by a weak civilian government and by revolutionary forces at home.

These resentments meant that the new Weimar Republic – which signed the peace treaty – lacked support. In 1922-23 the German economy collapsed after paying excessive war reparations, and then collapsed again after 1929 during the Great Depression. This helped Adolf Hitler and the right-wing National Socialist (Nazi) Party gain power with a promise to tear up the treaty and re-arm Germany.

AGGRIEVED NATIONS

Other countries were also angered by the settlement. Italy had not gained all the territory promised to it by the Allies when it joined the war in 1915. Japan too felt cheated by its meagre gains in the Pacific. Austria was angry because it was forbidden to unite with Germany, despite the wishes of its people. France believed Germany had not been punished enough, while Soviet Russia was not even included in the peace settlement and felt excluded from international affairs.

Above all, the new map of Europe still left many peoples living under foreign rule: millions of Hungarians lived in Romania and elsewhere, while a third of Poland's inhabitants were not even Polish. In the Middle East, the Arabs of Iraq, Syria and Palestine went from Ottoman to British or French rule and were denied independence. Almost everywhere, the peace treaties caused as many problems as they solved.

LONG-TERM CONSEQUENCES

The failure of the peace settlement became evident in 1939, when Germany invaded Poland, starting World War Two. Other aggrieved nations, notably Italy and Japan, later joined in the war. Britain and France struggled to resist, but they had failed to recover their strength after the conflict of 1914-18. Only the US had emerged from that war in better shape than it had gone in. And while it was not clear in 1919, it was obvious by 1945 that the US was now a world power.

"Those who sign this Treaty will sign the death sentence of many millions of German men, women and children."

Count Ulrich von Brockdorff-Rantzau, head of German delegation to Versailles

The Post-War World

February 1919 National Constituent Assembly meets in Weimar, Germany, to agree new constitution, setting up the Weimar Republic.

March 1919 League of Nations established at Geneva in neutral Switzerland.

March 1919 Austrian parliament votes for *Anschluss* (union) with Germany, later forbidden by the peace treaties.

June 1919 German delegation told to sign Treaty of Versailles or face renewed war.

June 1919 Treaty of Versailles signed.

November 1919 US Senate rejects Treaty of Versailles.

August 1922 German currency collapses, causing hyper-inflation and severe economic hardship in Germany.

April 1924 Dawes Plan for repaying reparations stabilises German economy.

October 1929 New York Stock Exchange crashes, causing worldwide economic catastrophe.

January 1933 Adolf Hitler comes to power in Germany.

September 1939 Germany invades Poland to regain land lost at Versailles, starting World War Two.

GLOSSARY

Alliance A formal agreement or pact, often military, between two or more nations.

Allies, the Britain, France, Russia and the other nations, including the United States, who fought on the same side in World War One.

Annexe To take over a territory by conquest or occupation.

Armistice An agreement between opposing sides to cease fire while a peace settlement is agreed.

Artillery Heavy guns, such as mortars, cannon and so on, used to attack an enemy line.

Autocrat A ruler who possesses absolute and unrestricted power and authority in his country.

Central Powers Germany, Austria-Hungary, Bulgaria and the Ottoman Empire, who fought as allies in World War One.

Colony A region or country controlled by another country as part of an empire.

Communism A belief in a society that exists without different social classes and in which everyone is equal and all property is owned by the people.

Conscript A person who is enrolled compulsorily for military service.

Constitution A statement, document or series of laws agreed by parliament covering all the basic principles on which the country is to be governed and spelling out the rights of its citizens.

Empire A large area of land made up of different countries and peoples, ruled by one nation and its emperor.

Entente An agreement or understanding between two or more countries.

Front An area where two opposing armies face each other, also known as the front line.

Genocide The deliberate killing of one nationality or ethnic group by another, as occurred to the Armenians in the Ottoman Empire in 1915.

Great powers The major nations of the world, such as Germany and Britain.

Infantry Soldiers who fight on foot.

Mandate A former German colony or Ottoman territory given to Allies under ultimate responsibility of the League of Nations in order to be prepared for eventual independence.

Mobilise To prepare an army for war; a general mobilisation includes all the armed services and many civilian services.

Mutiny An open rebellion by soldiers or seamen against their officers, usually punishable by death.

Neutral A nation that refuses to take sides in a war and does not fight.

Ratify To give formal approval in parliament to a treaty or agreement.

Recruit A person who joins an army voluntarily.

Reparations Financial compensation paid by the losers to the winners of a war.

Treaty A formal agreement between two or more countries.

Ultimatum A final demand by one government to another insisting that it agrees with all the terms and conditions set forth.

INDEX